This organ by A. Ruth & Son of Germany is a very loud instrument. Several of this make may be heard in Britain in museums or at summer outdoor rallies.

MECHANICAL MUSIC

Kevin McElhone

Shire Publications Ltd

CONTENTS

Published in 1997 by Shire Publications Ltd, Cromwell House, Church Street, Princes Risborough, Buckinghamshire HP27 9AA, UK. Copyright © 1997 by Kevin McElhone. First published 1997. Shire Album 333. ISBN 0 7478 0354 4. Kevin McElhone is hereby identified as the author of this work in accordance with Section 77 of the Copyright, Designs and Patents Act 1988.

Printed in Great Britain by CIT Printing Services, Press Buildings, Merlins Bridge, Haverfordwest, Pembrokeshire SA61 1XF.

British Library Cataloguing in Publication Data. McElhone, Kevin. Mechanical Music. – (Shire album; 333) 1. Musical instruments (Mechanical) 2. Musical instruments (Mechanical) – History I. Title 786.6 ISBN 0 7478 0354 4

Cover. Top left: *The 20 note Gem cob organ was made in hundreds of thousands; like most other sizes of organette, it played only tunes made by the company which made the instrument.* Top right: *A table-top Symphonion disc-playing musical box with disc removed to show the two tuned combs which are played in this popular small home model.* Bottom left: *One of two main types of violin player, the Phonolist played one string on each of three violins and was pneumatically operated on top of the player piano which accompanied it.* Bottom right: *An Aeolian Orchestrelle model V, serial number 7077, built in about 1904, at Keith Harding's World of Mechanical Music, Northleach, Gloucestershire.*

ACKNOWLEDGEMENTS

My thanks to my wife, Sheila, for helping translate the intricacies of mechanical music into something that can be understood by all.

The Aeolian organ diagram (page 26, top) comes from the book *The Barrel Organ* by Arthur W. J. G. Ord-Hume and the diagram showing how the disc musical box works (page 9, top) comes from *The Musical Box* by the same author. Both illustrations are the copyright of Arthur W. J. G. Ord-Hume and the Library of Mechanical Music and Horology. The player piano diagram (page 15, top) was drawn by Julian Dyer, editor of the Player Piano Group magazine. Three illustrations from the Rye Treasury of Mechanical Music (page 8, top right; page 18, bottom; page 19, top) were provided by Mr Mike Boyd. All other illustrations are either photographs taken by Ted Brown, the author or original advertisements dating from c.1895-1920.

THE RUDOLPH WURLITZER COMPANY, CINCINNATI - CHICAGO.   30

MILITARY BAND ORGAN.   (Style 125—44 Keys.)

Case finished in Imitation Walnut or Rosewood, with Engraved Scroll Work Gilded. This can also be furnished in Quartered White Oak.

Operated by Perforated Paper Rolls.

A Wurlitzer military band organ: an original advertisement of around 1910. The British equivalent of its price of $775 was about £200, which at the time would have paid for a small house!

Automatic musical instruments

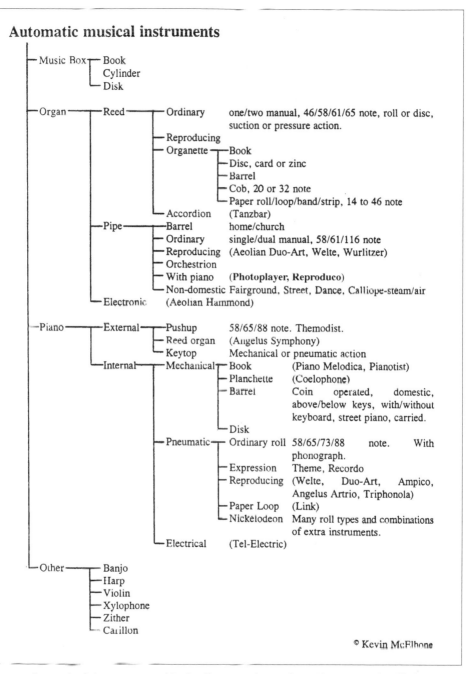

- Music Box
  - Book
  - Cylinder
  - Disk
- Organ
  - Reed
    - Ordinary — one/two manual, 46/58/61/65 note, roll or disc, suction or pressure action.
    - Reproducing
    - Organette
      - Book
      - Disc, card or zinc
      - Barrel
      - Cob, 20 or 32 note
      - Paper roll/loop/band/strip, 14 to 46 note
    - Accordion — (Tanzbar)
  - Pipe
    - Barrel — home/church
    - Ordinary — single/dual manual, 58/61/116 note
    - Reproducing — (Aeolian Duo-Art, Welte, Wurlitzer)
    - Orchestrion
    - With piano — (**Photoplayer, Reproduco**)
    - Non-domestic — Fairground, Street, Dance, Calliope-steam/air
  - Electronic — (Aeolian Hammond)
- Piano
  - External
    - Pushup — 58/65/88 note. Themodist.
    - Reed organ — (Angelus Symphony)
    - Keytop — Mechanical or pneumatic action
  - Internal
    - Mechanical
      - Book — (Piano Melodica, Pianotist)
      - Planchette — (Coelophone)
      - Barrel — Coin operated, domestic, above/below keys, with/without keyboard, street piano, carried.
      - Disk
    - Pneumatic
      - Ordinary roll — 58/65/73/88 note. With phonograph.
      - Expression — Theme, Recordo
      - Reproducing — (Welte, Duo-Art, Ampico, Angelus Artrio, Triphonola)
      - Paper Loop — (Link)
      - Nickelodeon — Many roll types and combinations of extra instruments.
    - Electrical — (Tel-Electric)
- Other
  - Banjo
  - Harp
  - Violin
  - Xylophone
  - Zither
  - Carillon

Automatic musical instruments: this family tree shows the wide range of self-playing instruments that have been made since about the middle of the eighteenth century.

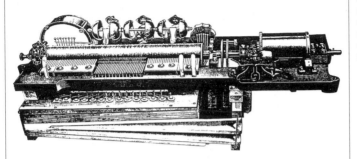

The movement from an expensive orchestral musical box which plays tuned combs, reed organ, drum, castanets and six bells. There was also the option of changing the cylinder for a different one.

MUSICAL BOXES

In Switzerland in 1796 Antoine Favre patented a musical watch which played tuned steel reeds. Favre intended his invention only for indoor use. It began as a quiet domestic instrument, which was later developed into musical boxes which had a steel tooth that was plucked to produce the characteristic and enchanting sound.

Early boxes were made by watchmakers and were wound by a key, like that for a clock, which could be used when a flap at the end of the box had been opened. The key wound a clockwork spring which, via a system of gearing and a speed governor, caused a pinned cylinder to rotate and pluck the teeth. Early boxes had many more teeth than later ones. They were very thin, fine and close together, which meant that often there was space for only three or four tunes.

Keys were easily lost but technical advances were made so that by the middle of the nineteenth century a musical box would be wound by a lever which was permanently attached to the instrument. Teeth were originally made singly or in small groups of a few together so that an early box might actually be playing many combs, as they were later called, all placed so close to each other that they appeared to be one. Later the comb was made from a single piece of steel with about fifty to a hundred teeth in it. These teeth were much further apart, allowing more tunes, often up to ten, to be pinned on one cylinder.

The box was started and played one tune. The cylinder then moved up a fraction of an inch while it continued to revolve past a blank area at the end of the first tune and the start of the second. It played all the tunes in sequence before being returned to the start by a spring when the last tune had finished. The programme of tunes would be listed on an ornate tune card fixed to the lid of the box.

Early boxes simply had a single musical

4

Right: *The movement in this late box has a double spring which allows it to play for over thirty minutes on one winding. Note the widely spaced teeth, which allow ten tunes on this box.*

Above: *A typical handwritten tune card listing the programme, or Gamme as it was called. Many makers made the same Gamme over many years on many different sizes of mechanisms.*

Right: *Thorens is the only firm producing new disc boxes today in Switzerland. They are of two sizes: this is the 4½ inch (11.4 cm) mechanism, the smallest disc size ever made, driven by teeth on the edge of the disc.*

An unusual view from the rear of a 15½ inch (39.4 cm) coin-operated Polyphon with soundboard removed, clearly showing the coin chute, the combs and the disc in position ready to play.

comb, but later examples were made with two combs. The second comb had teeth tuned at a slightly different frequency from the other comb; this gave a wavering effect called 'sublime harmony'. Boxes with three combs were also made; with good arrangements this could give an effect called 'forte-piano'. Thus it would play quietly on one comb which had relatively soft teeth, and then much louder on another comb which had much harder teeth, so by combining soft, loud or both there were three 'volume settings', as they might be called today. The third comb was used to accent particular passages in the piece of music by playing either louder or in harmony with either of the other combs. Each of the combs would often have more than one tooth tuned to the same pitch, so there might actually be six teeth in the musical box which played the same note at three different volume or loudness levels, and any number of teeth could be plucked at the same time.

Later on the manufacturers tried to persuade their wealthy customers that they must have additional instruments in their box. So drums and wooden blocks were added as accompaniment, and so too were tuned bells. These were often highly engraved and were played by ornate strikers in the shape of butterflies, bees or people. Small reed-organ sections were also added and there are some boxes that play just these organ reeds and do not have a musical comb. The notes played on the drum, bell or other attachment were pinned on a particular section of the revolving cylinder and could often be turned off by moving a lever. Some makers added a 'zither', which was a piece of tissue-type paper. This changed the sound of the teeth and could be lowered into a playing position at random.

In the mid nineteenth century, before the invention of gramophones and radio, the owners of musical boxes had at their command the only method then available of hearing a pre-recorded programme of music. Those who could not play an instrument and thus make their own music would have had very quiet evenings unless they bought a musical box, and it became quite fashionable to play the musical box to visiting friends. However, they would soon grow tired of listening to the same few tunes. The obvious solution was to be able to change the cylinder and thereby the selection of tunes available. So interchangeable cylinder boxes were made, often with very fancy stands or tables containing the extra cylinders.

These boxes were very expensive and a much cheaper way of changing a tune

A good example of a musical box trade card sent or given to potential customers in the late nineteenth century.

was needed. In 1886 Paul Lochmann of Leipzig, Germany, produced the first commercially successful disc-playing musical box, which was marketed as the Symphonion. Round flat discs made at first of zinc, and later of stronger steel, had projections punched into them and these plucked a 'star wheel', which in turn plucked the tuned tooth in the musical comb. Two of the workers in this company left and set up the Polyphonmusikwerke, which made an instrument called the Polyphon. This name is often used today as the generic term for all disc-playing musical boxes. Within a few years many different companies were producing a wide range of models in Europe, the United States and elsewhere.

The smallest size of disc was 4¹/₂ inches (11.4 cm) and the largest was 32 inches (81.3 cm). As with the cylinder-type boxes, there were various combinations of combs ranging from single to double in table-top models. The large upright coin-in-the-slot models intended for use in public places might have up to four combs.

Most families bought small table-top models which had discs usually up to 15 inches (38.1 cm) in diameter, although some were as big as 27 inches (68.6 cm). Discs were mass-produced, being copied from a master plate. All the popular tunes from recent London or Broadway shows were available, as well as traditional dances and music-hall songs.

The more expensive upright coin-

This selection of discs shows Regina and Polyphon 15¹/₂ inch (39.4 cm) musical box discs above and German made Amorette and Ariston organette discs below.

MUSICAL BOXES.

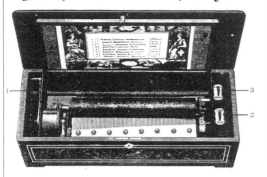

EXPLANATIONS FOR USING MUSICAL BOXES.

TO WIND UP, use Lever marked No. 1.
TO START, pull forward No. 2.
TO STOP AT THE END OF THE TUNE, push backwards No. 2.
TO CHANGE THE TUNE, push back No. 3.
TO REPEAT THE SAME TUNE, pull forward No. 3 while the tune you wish to have repeated is playing.

Attachment for changing tune at will, may be ordered with larger boxes. It is then found between the large Cylinder wheel and lever No. 3. To obtain any tune on the list, stop the box at the end of the air, then pull the attachment forward the necessary number of times, until the Indicator shows the desired tune.

SPEED REGULATOR. - This attachment consists of a lever at the right of the escapement, between the latter and lever No. 2. When it is pulled toward the front of the instrument, the movement will run at its slowest; when the lever is pushed backward, the tune is rendered in a faster tempo.

IMPORTANT. — In order to have the speed regulator work satisfactorily, it is indispensable that the right side of the wheel nearest the cylinder wheel be occasionally oiled, so as to avoid wearing by friction.

When not used the box must always be stopped AT THE END OF A TUNE, as otherwise the delicate dampers under the teeth of the comb will be damaged, and the music in consequence be marred by a squeaking and scratching noise. STRICT ATTENTION IS CALLED TO THIS RULE.

Above left: *How to use the cylinder musical box, from an original catalogue of around 1890.*

Above right: *This coin-operated Polyphon musical box plays steel discs which are 19⅝ inches (50 cm) in diameter. It was one of the most popular sizes made and was used in public houses and elsewhere. This example is at the Rye Treasury of Mechanical Music in East Sussex.*

Left: *This unusual type of musical box, popularly called a 'Capital Cuff', plays sleeves or cuffs, as collectors have named the music. Each hollow sleeve is a cross between a disc and a cylinder, rather like a cheese grater, and is easily changed, as can be seen in this example which has ten music sheets in all.*

operated models were quite loud and some had bells added. When fully wound the larger models could play for forty-five minutes, but someone still had to remove the disc and replace it with a different title, which was not ideal in a public place. So the final development of the coin-operated disc musical box was the auto-changer, an enormous machine which had a rack in the bottom containing up to twelve discs. The desired tune was selected by turning a lever and when the coin had been inserted in the slot the disc would automatically be loaded, played and then returned into the storage rack. This is a very early example of a 'juke-box', long before the term was first coined.

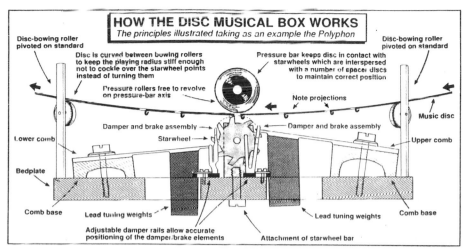

HOW THE DISC MUSICAL BOX WORKS
The principles illustrated taking as an example the Polyphon

Disc-bowing roller pivoted on standard

Disc is curved between bowing rollers to keep the playing radius stiff enough not to cockle over the starwheel points instead of turning them

Pressure rollers free to revolve on pressure-bar axis

Pressure bar keeps disc in contact with starwheels which are interspersed with a number of spacer discs to maintain correct position

Disc-bowing roller pivoted on standard

Note projections

Music disc

Lower comb

Damper and brake assembly

Starwheel

Damper and brake assembly

Upper comb

Bedplate

Comb base

Lead tuning weights

Lead tuning weights

Comb base

Adjustable damper rails allow accurate positioning of the damper/brake elements

Attachment of starwheel bar

Above: *This side view of a Polyphon musical box with the disc in the playing position shows how the disc projections turn the starwheel, which then plucks the teeth on the two combs. (From 'The Musical Box' by Arthur W. J. G. Ord-Hume.)*

Right: *Some cylinder musical boxes were used in public places. This one, used in France, required 10 centimes to play a tune and has a very long playing spring. Most coin-operated musical boxes played discs.*

Below: *An unusual Troubadour disc musical box with a good example of the kind of illustration used on the lid of these instruments.*

Right: *A very small, cheap two-tune cylinder movement is shown here in the back of a Victorian musical photograph album. These were made in large numbers. When the clasp which held the album shut when not in use was opened, the music played.*

STREET INSTRUMENTS

In the late nineteenth century the average person could not hope to own a mechanical musical instrument himself because of the relatively high cost, but there was a vast selection of instruments to listen to in the street.

The earliest instrument used in the street was called, incorrectly, a 'barrel organ' in Britain or a 'hurdy-gurdy' in the United States, but it was actually a small barrel-operated dulcimer. It was a wooden-framed machine, with strings like a piano, and was carried around by the 'musician', with a strap round his neck and a wooden support leg under the instrument. The best-remembered maker was Joseph Hicks of Bristol, who made instruments which played eight songs on 22 to 27 notes. These instruments were often out of tune, as a result of the variable British weather, to the extent that rich people

would pay the grinder to move down the street away from their homes!

Later on, much larger street barrel pianos were made, some just with strings, others with added bells, wood blocks or a device called a tremolo which gave a re-iterating sound to each note played. They too had wooden frames, and when in good order they could produce a lovely haunting sound, like all fully restored and well-cared-for instruments today. They were usually hired out by the day or the week, and the tunes were changed every so often by installing a different barrel, which contained up to ten tunes, mostly popular tunes of the day, but also some hymns. The barrel piano for street use was powered by turning a handle manually, which was hard work, whereas barrel pianos for indoor use in public places were powered by clockwork and started by inserting an old penny.

Left: A Hicks street barrel piano, dating from 1840-60, with 27 notes and eight different tunes. It would have been carried around the streets hanging by a strap round the operator's neck.

Below: The smallest hand-turned roll-driven street organ is the standard 20 note. This example was made in the 1970s by Hofbauer in Germany and is loud for its size.

Right: *There are several hundred preserved fairground organs still playing throughout the world. Many are found in Britain; this example is being powered by electricity generated by a steam showman's locomotive.*

Below: *It takes ninety turns of the handle to play any of the ten tunes, each lasting about one minute, on this forty-key street barrel piano, made by Tomasso in London.*

Below: *A close-up of the heart of the organ, showing the bellows at the bottom and many pipes, each row or rank giving a different type of sound.*

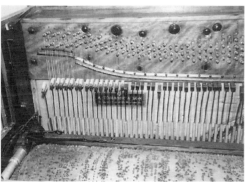

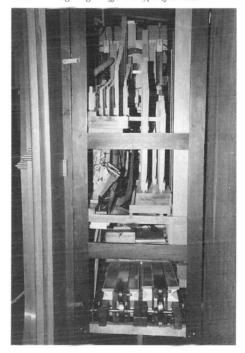

Many street musicians with hand-turned Hicks-type or larger barrel pianos or organs had a small pet monkey which not only amused the children but also shook a small tin to encourage passers-by to 'drop a copper in', a copper being an old penny coin. The animal was often dressed up in a small coat and a hat, to protect it from the cold climate.

The larger barrel organ was used in the streets and also in fairgrounds but, having only a few tunes on expensive barrels, it soon became obsolete. In 1892 Anselme Gavioli first successfully used a folding cardboard 'book' for a fairground organ. This enabled unlimited tunes to be played and cost much less than a replacement barrel. Fairground organs grew to enormous proportions, many having several hundred pipes, and were claimed to produce sound equivalent to that of a large orchestra. They were used on all kinds of rides and also at the fairground bioscope shows, where silent films were shown

Right: *The inside of a modern small Spanish barrel piano, with the barrel removed, clearly showing the triangle, wood block and individual hammers.*

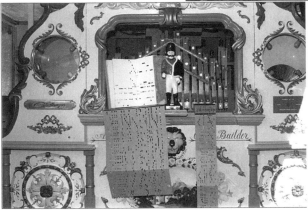

Left: *This photograph shows the 'book' music used by many instruments: (top left) Piano Melodico 30 note; (bottom left) Gavioli 89 key fair organ; (right) 30 note fair organ. They are hanging, for photographic purposes only, on the front of a David Leach organ, built recently in 1980, owned by Dave Parriss in Wellingborough.*

before static cinemas were set up.

In many European countries much smaller hand-turned street organs were used, with both cardboard book music and paper rolls. A large number were used in the Netherlands and Germany. Some contained pipes and others contained reeds, which were quieter but stayed in tune much longer. The smallest of these instruments had only twenty notes, so that they were easily moved around the streets of larger towns and cities. Musicians often sang along to the popular or traditional folk tunes for added entertainment and as an extra inducement for people to part with their money.

In their most advanced form these organs had drums, bells, accordions and lighting effects. Some were also used indoors, in dance halls, particularly in the Low Countries. The cardboard book passed over a keyframe which read the holes punched in it. As a hole appeared, a key rose up and via linkages and valves opened up a pallet at the bottom of the pipe. This allowed air to rush out of the reservoir where it was stored, through the pipe, making the sound. The books also controlled which rows or ranks of pipes were to play, such as loud trumpet, softer violins, flute sounds, and also drums and other percussion. Large organs which played paper rolls used a method to read them almost the same as the vacuum system used in the player piano, although pipes are always sounded by air under pressure.

Fairground organs generally continued in use until replaced by recorded music, which is much cheaper to run and easier to transport. There are today numerous small firms which still make outdoor organs, from 20 notes up to 90 notes, and they also continue to make new music rolls and books. A few owners of vintage fairground rides have even purchased new organs to replace ones which were removed from their rides in the 1940s or 1950s.

PLAYER PIANOS

The first self-playing domestic pianos were operated by barrels, like the street pianos, but they rarely had more than two barrels with them and thus had a limited repertoire. Attempts were first made by Alexandre Debain in France around 1860 to make a piano which played flat wooden cards, called *planchettes*, which had pins sticking out of them to operate a key-frame on top of the piano. While this piano had a wider range of tunes available, it did not become popular.

The first successful means of playing a standard domestic piano automatically was to use an instrument called a 'Pianola', which was invented by Edwin Votey in 1896 and was built in Detroit in the United States. This very large machine contained sixty-five felt-covered wooden fingers within its case; when lined up with the piano keyboard, these could press the keys down in the same way as

the pianist. There was a paper music roll similar to those which had been available for player reed organs for over ten years. The foot treadles were simply pressed to create a vacuum in the main reservoir on the instrument, and when a hole passed over the tracker bar the hole was read. A valve then opened and a small pneumatic motor moved, causing the 'finger' to press down the piano key, thereby sounding the note.

These types of add-on machine are often called 'pushups' today because they had to be pushed up to the piano in order to play them, and they had to be removed to a corner of the room when the piano was to be played by hand. The largest maker of any kind of self-playing piano in the world was the Aeolian Corporation in the United States. They had showrooms throughout the world and bought all the rights to Edwin Votey's Pianola. They

A very useful player piano was the Marshall & Rose instrument built in 1909 at the time of the changeover from 65 to 88 note sizes of rolls as the industry standard. It plays both kinds of roll on two tracker bars. The bottom one is covered up by a strip of cloth when not in use.

This advertisement shows that using endorsements to sell is not a new idea. Aeolian marketed player pianos, reed and pipe organs in this way.

were so successful that the name 'Pianola'
was frequently used to describe any self-
playing piano.

Other companies quickly tried to copy
Aeolian's success by producing instruments with clockwork motors to drive the
roll and other labour-saving ideas to make
their models more desirable. They all used
advertising a great deal to try to convince
potential customers that their instrument
was the best. The Wilcox & White company even produced a pushup which also
contained a reed organ, thereby allowing
duets to be played (provided the piano
was tuned to the pitch of the organ first).
Instruments of this type were expensive
and took up a lot of space.

It was not until 1901 that Melville

This diagram and explanation of the operation of the player piano are reproduced by courtesy of Julian Dyer, editor of the Player Piano Group Bulletin. The pianola is powered by suction, provided by foot pedals. The music is provided by paper rolls which have holes punched in them to represent the tune. The roll passes over a bar (called the tracker bar) which contains a series of holes, one for each note. A note is played when a hole in the roll admits air into the hole in the tracker bar. This works as follows:
Initially, with the paper roll covering the tracker bar, suction through the bleed (a small hole, much smaller than the hole in the tracker bar) means that there is the

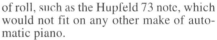

same air pressure on both sides of the pouch. The pouch is an airtight sheet of very thin flexible leather, and with the same air pressure on both sides it allows the valve to drop. The valve acts as a switch between the suction and the outside air, and when it is in its bottom position it allows air into the pneumatic. The pneumatic is a small bellows, and when air is allowed in, it drops open under gravity. So, in the normal state when the paper roll does not have a hole in it, the pianola mechanism does not touch the piano action.*
When a hole in the paper roll uncovers the tracker bar hole, it causes air to flow under the pouch, which therefore balloons upwards (as it still has suction above it). This pushes the valve upwards, admitting suction to the pneumatic, which is thus sucked shut. The push-rod attached to the pneumatic comes into contact with the piano action and plays the note.

Clarke produced the first piano containing the automatic parts inside, dispensing with the need for a 'pushup' machine. Therefore for the first time it was possible to play along with the roll on the piano's own keyboard.

The early instruments played only 58 notes of the keyboard, the same as the player reed organs which were being made, but later on 65 note instruments were made. The piano had any number of keys between 65 and 88 and so many of the notes could not be played from the music roll, and this was inadequate for the proper rendition of many classical tunes without adapting them to fit in only 65 notes instead of the full 88 notes on a normal full-sized piano keyboard. Different manufacturers made their own sizes

of roll, such as the Hupfeld 73 note, which would not fit on any other make of automatic piano.

Finally, after a convention in 1908, the industry adopted 88 note rolls as the standard type to be used in future. Makers started producing instruments with two tracker bars capable of playing both 65 and 88 note rolls. Indeed 65 note rolls were produced until about twenty years later but gradually lost popularity in favour of the new full-scale rolls. These

Right: The separate piano player unit, first called a pianola by the Aeolian Company, had sixty-five wooden fingers to play the keys of the piano. This 'orchestral' pushup by Wilcox & White in the USA could also play a duet as it contained organ reeds as well, but the piano had to be tuned to the same pitch as the organ.

15

dual-standard players are quite popular with enthusiasts today.

All of the rolls made at this stage were programmed on a drawing board and sounded rather mechanical as they were a direct copy from the sheet music and needed very skilful use of the controls of the player piano to get a realistic performance sounding like a live pianist. This soon changed when the reproducing piano was developed, first by Edwin Welte in

Right: Even grand pianos had player mechanisms fitted. This illustration of an 88 note Aeolian instrument comes from a French catalogue. Powered by the two pedals, it was educational and great fun to play.

Left: There were hundreds of companies making music rolls, but by 1920 only the biggest had survived to continue production over the final fifteen or so years of the heyday of such instruments.

Right: The ornate leaders at the start of each roll were almost an art form in themselves. They always claimed to be the best make.

16

Left: Reproducing pianos had their own rolls and their own recording artists for each main brand of player system. This advertisement claims the endorsement of some of the popular composers of the period 1900-20.

Below: All proper player piano (and organ) stools had sloping tops to ease the back muscles of the players, and many had storage bins for rolls underneath.

Germany and later by companies in the United States.

A great variety of systems was produced but all had the common feature that they played rolls which were recorded by contemporary pianists such as Edvard Grieg, Percy Grainger, Sergey Rachmaninov and so on. The pianist sat at a recording piano and as he played a master roll of paper was marked by pens with the notes played. This was then cut out by hand and checked, and then a machine produced a normal roll which could be played on the piano and would reproduce the sound exactly as created by the pianist. Some half-way systems called expression pianos had five different levels

17

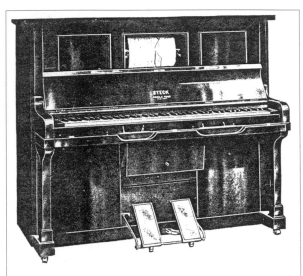

STECK UPRIGHT 'PIANOLA' PIANO

(British Manufacture)

FOOT-OPERATED 'DUO-ART'
MODEL 9 H

With Themodist, Metrostyle, and Automatic Sustaining Pedal Device. In Light or Dark Mahogany, Oak, Walnut or Black Case . . . .

Price 275 Guineas

:: DISCOUNT FOR CASH ::

of volume at which they played, but the real reproducing systems had many more: Duo-Art had sixteen, for example.

The principal systems were Red and Green Welte in Germany, Duo-Art and Ampico in the United States and Britain. There were several others but they did not become popular and most piano makers installed inside their pianos player systems which played these common types of roll. The actual pneumatic technology used to create loud and soft passages changed over the years, but basically there were perforations in the rolls which told the player mechanism how fast to push the hammers forwards on the piano, therefore controlling the volume.

Player pianos were made in very large numbers, with the peak of

This highly polished George Rogers grand player piano was made in the United States in 1925 and has the Ampico reproducing system in it. The mechanism was contained under the keyboard in a drawer which could be slid out to load a roll and pushed in out of the way when playing. The roll-drive motor is on the left and the various controls are at the front.

This strange-looking machine is the last original piano-roll punching machine in regular use in England. It was used by the Aeolian Company, and later by Artona in Ramsgate, Kent, and is currently used by the Universal Music Roll Company in Rye, East Sussex, to make new rolls, just the same as in the 1920s, but with the advantage of computer input, editing and recording.

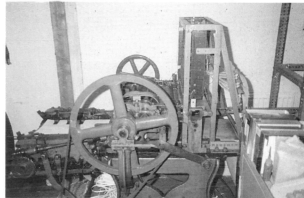

Two examples of the rare Golden tube roll adaptor. To avoid the need for a separate wooden spool for each piano roll, there was one spool which could be inserted through the centre of a roll mounted on a central core of card or brass. This saved both cost and space but did not catch on.

production being around 1923, but the gramophone was already taking over as the main provider of music in the home. The stock market crash of 1929 and the Depression brought about the end of most manufacturers by 1931 and nearly all by 1940. Rolls were made in their millions and there was an enormous range of music punched into paper, from Scott Joplin and jazz to ballads and classical concertos. Some companies had many thousands of titles available and were constantly adding the latest tunes and deleting out-of-date music from their catalogues.

Draper's 14 note organette was made in large numbers. This size was made by many companies worldwide and there was full compatibility of music rolls between different makes of this standard machine. This example has twin reeds.

INDOOR ORGANS

There was a successful attempt beginning during the mid 1880s to make small cheap organs for use in the home, and eventually an enormous range became available. These instruments were called organettes and were priced from a few shillings up to a few pounds. (A shilling comprised twelve old pence and was a twentieth part of a pound.) The smallest size was 14 notes, played from a paper music roll, and this became a standard size made by many different companies, with new tunes costing just a few pence.

These organettes were made in most countries in Europe as well as in the United States and even Japan. They nearly all played brass or steel reeds, like those used in a harmonium (if worked by pressure) or in an American organ (if worked by vacuum). They were simple to use and were often shown in advertisements as being suitable for use by children.

An idea of different note sizes and types

can be given by mentioning some of the popular instruments. The Aurephone had 17 notes; the Cabinetto or Tournaphone had 25. These were the same as the 14

The Tournaphone or Cabinetto played an enormous 25 note roll, 13 inches (33 cm) wide, often over 80 feet (24 metres) long. It had a swell flap in the lid for loud and soft passages and sold widely.

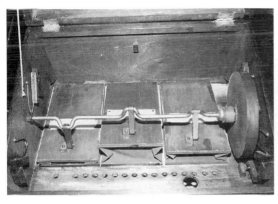

Above: *There were usually two, three or four exhausters inside an organette to produce an even supply of air because, although the reeds were on a low pressure, they used a high volume.*

Right: *A selection of rolls used by various table-top organettes: (from the left) 14 note English, 20 note Celestina, 25 note Cabinetto.*

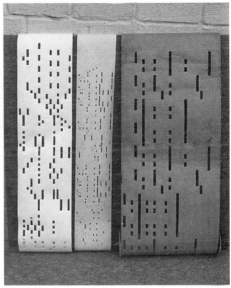

note organs, where at a hole in the roll the air was sucked into the reservoir by the vacuum created in it by turning the handle. It then passed over the metal reed and caused it to sound. It was so simple that many of these instruments are still working over a hundred years later.

The more complicated models had very small valves similar to those in a player piano. Examples of this type are the Celestina and the Seraphone, both of which played 20 note rolls which had from one to six tunes on them.

Each country developed its own ideas and each maker produced instruments which were declared to be superior in tone to anything else currently available. The Autophone company of Ithaca in the United States produced a very loud miniature barrel organette called a Gem Roller Organ in 1885. It was so popular and sold in such large numbers that the term 'roller organ' was often used in America to describe all table-top automatic reed organs. The barrel was 6 inches (15 cm) long and called a 'cob', as it was similar in size to a corn cob. It was pinned in a spiral so that it rotated three times in order to play the tune,

Above: *The Aurephone is a small 17 note organette similar to the Cabinetto in that the paper simply uncovers the reed, thereby allowing the air to rush across its surface, as in a mouth-organ.*

which lasted about one minute. Early examples worked by pressure, later ones by vacuum. They also produced the Grand Roller Organ, which had a larger barrel, 13 inches (33 cm) long, rotating eight times in order to play a tune on 32 notes, with a duration of around three minutes.

Right: *The popular
Celestina played a 20 note
paper roll and endless
bands of music and had
small valves and pouches
like a player piano. The
rolls were used by similar
machines made by other
companies such as the
Seraphone.*

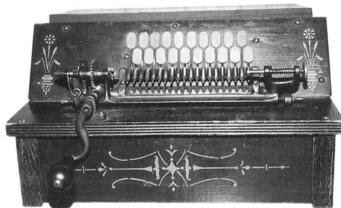

Left: *Unfortunately
most other sizes of
organette allowed
the playing only of
tunes made by the
company which
made the instru-
ment, such as the
clever 20 note Gem
cob organ, made in
hundreds of
thousands.*

Right: *The larger Grand
Roller Organ of 32 notes,
'ideal for the large home or
small church', offered a
choice, eventually, of two
hundred pieces of music. 20
and 32 note cobs are shown
for size comparison.*

In Germany many models such as the 22 or 39 note Mignon played paper rolls. The Manopan played 22 or 39 note folding cardboard books. The most popular models played circular discs. The Ariosa and Amorette played zinc doughnut-shaped rings and zinc discs respectively, rather like disc musical boxes. The Ariston organette played flat cardboard discs on 19, 24 and 36 note models using a system of metal keys to read the holes, just like on the keyed fairground organs.

There were many variations, and some models had dancing dolls, bells, drums, glockenspiel bars or additional sets of reeds to enhance the music. Some were made to last, while others were made of softwood which was soon destroyed by woodworm if left forgotten in later years.

Listening to the organette was often quite a family occasion, as apart from playing an instrument oneself it was the

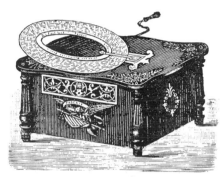

Ariosa-Phönix mit 18 Stahlstimmen *M* 16.—, doppeltönig *M* 24.—. Notenblätter à *M* —.60.

Phönix in schwarz polirtem Kasten, 44 Cm. lang, 33 Cm. breit, 25 Cm. hoch, mit 24 Stimmen **M. 32.50.** doppeltönig . . . . „ 60.—.

only way to hear music in the home. In the days before electricity or cars an organette was one of the few status symbols a family could possess.

Since the late eighteenth century there had been chamber barrel organs. They worked like their street-organ cousins but had pipes which were voiced to a much quieter level. They often had a cupboard with several extra barrels and were quite robust. Indeed Admiral Parry took one with him on an Arctic expedition as the only entertainment on the ship.

There was also a whole family of indoor automatic reed organs of similar size to a harmonium and much larger. Around 1889 an organ that played a 46 note paper roll was introduced, to be followed in 1891 by one called the Aeolian Grand which played 58 note paper rolls, although it

A typical French indoor barrel organ made in the late nineteenth century. Some barrels contained hymns and some secular tunes, often accompanied by drum and triangle.

Right: *This model 'S' Orchestrelle played the standard 58 note roll and worked on vacuum like a player piano.*

Below: *This solo Orchestrelle model XY plays 58 and 116 note rolls which operate two manuals like a pipe organ. It works on air under pressure both to read the roll and to play the notes.*

had 73 notes on the keyboard. These organs were very loud but were capable of playing almost any kind of music from ragtime to organ sonatas. The Aeolian Company later introduced a very large range of pressure-operated organs called the Orchestrelle, playing 58 and later 116 note rolls. These instruments were up to 8 feet (2.44 metres) high and the top of the range models were extremely expensive.

Wilcox & White produced a range of vacuum-operated instruments and also the combination piano player and reed organ already mentioned. Most makers of reed organs produced their own player models, such as the Bellolian by Bell of Guelph in Canada, but they were not popular and only three examples of this particular make are known to have survived. Storey & Clark made a player reed organ with a clockwork rewind motor, and Malcolm & Company in England made the 61 note Phoneon. All the others mentioned were 58 note. Mustel in France even produced a model which would play 88 note piano rolls, and Schiedmayer in Germany made one which was accompanied by a glockenspiel.

The largest organs made for indoor use were called residence pipe organs, and these were mostly put into the mansions of the very wealthy. Basically the

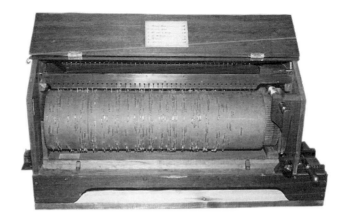

Right: *A 'dumb or-ganist' was placed over the top of a standard organ key-board and enabled a church temporarily without a human organist to have music to sing to. Wooden rods (Pit-mans) pushed the keys down. There were usually only six or eight tunes on a barrel.*

Below: *This barrel-operated player pipe organ was made by Welte & Sons in Germany for use in the home and commer-cially. It stood 12 feet 9 inches (3.89 metres) high, and accord-ing to the original advertisement it 'replaces a complete brass band of thirty-five men'.*

same as the pipe organs found in churches, they were voiced in a different way to suit the wider range of music available on paper rolls. Aeolian made models which played 116 note rolls, that is two manuals of 58 notes each (each keyboard is called a manual), and the operator controlled all of the stops by hand and also the swell shut-ters for loud and soft. They also produced a fully auto-matic organ which used rolls with 176 holes in them, called Duo-Art (not to be confused with piano rolls of the same name), which controlled all of the stop and swell settings from the roll. Other makers were Kimball, Estey, Moller and Wurlitzer in the United States and Welte in Germany. Many of these organs have been destroyed, but there are about twenty-six left in Brit-ain, of which several can still be heard today.

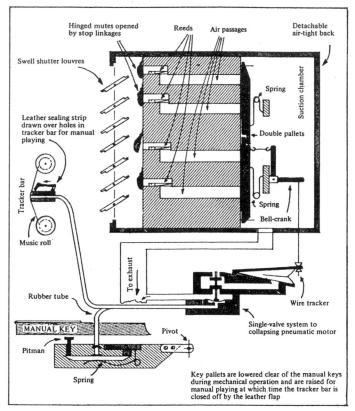

Left: *This shows the principle of operation of the early suction models of the Aeolian 58 note reed organ. (From 'The Barrel Organ' by Arthur W. J. G. Ord-Hume.)*

Below right: *This is an early chamber barrel organ built by Joseph Davis of London between 1812 and 1829. It has 16 notes playing on one wooden and three metal sets or ranks of pipes, plus drum and triangle. It has one hymn and two secular barrels, each playing ten tunes.*

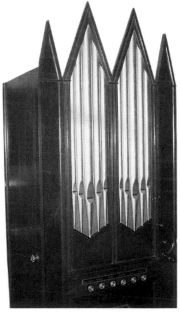

Below: *A Photoplayer had piano, organ, drums and many sound effects, from bird warbler to fire-engine bell, located in the two cabinets either side of the main instrument. They were used to accompany silent films and some could be operated by the projectionist by remote control.*

OTHER INSTRUMENTS

There was an amazing range of other instruments that were made to play automatically, including almost all of the popular types. Some were obviously for private use in the home, such as the Rollmonica, a mouth-organ. Others, like nickelodeons, were for use in public places.

The nickelodeon got its name from the fact that it cost a nickel (5 cents) to hear one tune. They were all based on a standard piano, usually with the addition of a mandolin rail, which was a set of metal tacks lowered between the piano hammers and the strings to alter the sound to a 'rinky tink' style. But many had up to ten extra instruments added, some for percussion such as drums, triangle, wood blocks and so forth, and others such as a xylophone or glockenspiel, or a rank of violin or flute organ pipes would take over the melody line for a time. Some instruments played one ten-tune roll, but the more advanced and expensive models had two spool boxes so that one roll could play while the other was rewinding or being changed. They had lighting effects and mostly played popular toe-tapping dance tunes of the day. Many were found in bars and when prohibition in the United States led to the closure of these establishments, the instruments fell out of use.

In Europe roll-operated orchestrions with pipes rather than a piano as the basic instrument were favoured, but the most unusual type was the violin-playing instrument. There were two main makes of these, the Phonolist, made in Germany by Hupfeld, and the Violano, made by the Mills Novelty Company in the United States. The Phonolist was operated pneumatically like a player piano and had three violins in a case on top of a normal piano. However, only one string of each violin was actually played from the roll. The Violano was electrically operated in every respect. The roll was read electrically and solenoids played the piano hammers and the single violin, which had four strings, all of which were played simultaneously.

Above: *A pocket-size instrument was the Rollmonica, a roll-operated mouth-organ, originally made in bakelite and more recently in bright plastic. This 12 note model takes a lot of blowing.*

Right: *A typical Seeburg nickelodeon, popular in the United States from 1905 to 1930. Most models had fancy glass in them, often lit from behind.*

27

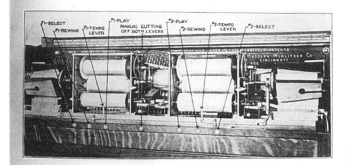

A twin spool box on a Wurlitzer nickelodeon enabled the machine to rewind one roll while playing another. It could therefore play non-stop, which was a valuable feature when in commercial use.

Right: *Most nickelodeons were automatic pianos with the addition of pipes, glockenspiel or, in this example, a xylophone.*

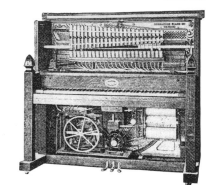

COINOLA

Style C-Xylophone Interior

The Style C case can be had with a choice of four installations. The Coinola trouble proof mechanism used in each will give years of satisfactory service and profits.

Style C, Regular (Piano and mandolin,) a regular 65-note installation using the "A" or 65-note roll.

Style C Xylophone. The best all around instrument made. Piano, mandolin and two octaves of Deagan Xylophone bars. Uses Solo "O" roll.

Style C Flute or Violin, piano, mandolin and either two octaves of flute pipes or two octaves of violin pipes. Uses Solo "O" Roll.

Left: *Said to be 'the eighth wonder of the world', the Mills Novelty Company's Violano was made in large numbers for operation mostly in public places. It always fascinated onlookers and still does.*

Left: This automatic zither, called a Triola, is a joy to hear. The roll plays 25 melody notes and the operator plays the accompaniment. Instructions as to whether to play a chord or to 'strum' are on the roll.

Below: The Wurlitzer Automatic Harp is another means of obtaining a tune from a string. They did not hold their tune for very long but were popular in roadside establishments in the USA.

Some rare Violano models had multiple violins or cellos, and one example had a keyboard from which the violin could be played, but these are not to be seen in Europe today.

Smaller instruments included musical clocks, some of which played sets of tuned bells, while some contained musical box cylinder or disc movements and others played a pipe organ operated by a barrel. There were also singing birds, which were usually in the form of a cage containing a feathered bird which moved in time to bird-like noises made by a mechanism in the base of the cage. The sound was created by a clockwork-powered set of bellows and a pipe with a slide on it which when moved up and down varied the pitch of the sound. These are all quite hard to find today, but there are some good collections to visit.

One of the larger automatic instruments is the carillon, which is usually but not always contained in a church. It basically comprises a barrel-operated set of church bells activated by the clock on the hour, although some are also playable by hand as well. The best ones are found in the Low Countries.

Small numbers of automatic harps were made by the Wurlitzer Company, as was a novelty called the Encore Banjo. This instrument had four strings which were plucked by four automatic plectrums. It

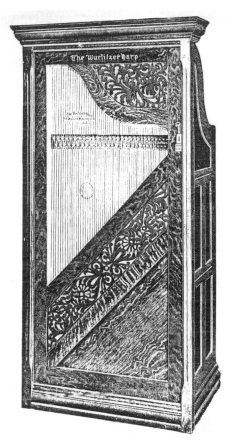

Right: *This Wurlitzer instrument combined a pipe organ on the upper, shorter keyboard with a piano on the lower keyboard.*

Left: *The mechanism of a 28 note Tanzbar roll-playing concertina. The holes are read by keys which can be seen sticking up in the centre of the instrument. It is very difficult to play as one must learn to reverse the squeezing of the instrument in between phrases in the music so that there are no silent pauses.*

played mainly popular tunes, contained on long rolls like most other coin-operated instruments.

Many manufacturers installed their machines in cafés or bars and shared the takings from these coin-operated instruments with the proprietors. The rolls would be changed every so often, as the latest tunes were superseded in popularity by more up-to-date ones.

There were a few roll-playing actual steam organs made in the United States, where they were called calliopes. They were very loud, some advertisements claiming that their sound could carry over one mile (1.6 km). They were not made in other countries but in Britain, confusingly, fairground organs are often called steam organs, the term originating in the days when a steam traction or showman's engine generated the electrical power to work the air bellows or rotary blower on the organs.

MUSICAL SOCIETIES

Mechanical music is an enormous subject and many people may be deterred from becoming involved in it as a hobby by its complexity and by fears that it will prove to be an expensive interest. But an unrestored instrument can be obtained quite cheaply and anyone who has some spare time, average practical skills and the ability to follow the instructions in a restoration manual should be able to restore it and thereby gain considerable satisfaction.

Some people collect audio recordings, which is certainly easier than having a 7 ton lorry with a large fairground organ in it. With so many museums to visit and societies to join, it is easy to get involved with a dedicated group of mechanical music enthusiasts. Many of the societies hold regular meetings: some are held in the homes of collectors, to listen to instruments, and some are at larger venues, when restoration tips and so forth may be obtained.

There are several societies which cater for a variety of instruments in the field of mechanical music, although some specialise in particular kinds. Their journals have articles on everything from acquisition and restoration to building new instruments. They have members who are experts in many areas and are able to offer advice. Joining any one of these societies should put the reader in touch with people who can answer any questions that may arise.

UNITED KINGDOM

British Organ Grinders Association (BOGA): membership details from Geoff Todd, telephone 01869 338532.

Fairground Organ Preservation Society (FOPS): 43 Woolmans, Fullers Slade, Milton Keynes, Buckinghamshire MK11 2BA.

Friends of the Pianola Institute: Mr Mike Davies, 9 Jillian Close, Chestnut Avenue, Hampton, Middlesex TW12 2NX.

Mechanical Organ Owners Society (MOOS): Field Head Farm, Outgate, Ambleside, Cumbria LA22 0PY.

Musical Box Society of Great Britain (MBSGB): Secretary, PO Box 299, Landbeach, Cambridge CB4 4PJ.

North West Player Piano Association (NWPPA): Mr Everson Whittle, 47 Raikes Road, Preston, Lancashire PR1 5EQ.

Player Piano Association of Wales and the West: 161 Longmead Avenue, Horfield, Bristol BS7 8QG.

Player Piano Group: Membership Secretary, 80 Montalt Road, Woodford Green, Essex IG8 9SS.

OTHER COUNTRIES

L'Association des Amis des Automates: M Christian Bailly, 1 Rue du Dahomey, 75011 Paris, France.

Australian Collectors of Mechanical Musical Instruments (ACMMI): Mr Ian Savins, 19 Waipori Street, St Ives 2075, Australia.

Automatic Musical Instrument Collectors Association (AMICA): Mr R. Pratt, 515 Scott Street, Sandusky, Ohio 44870-3736, USA.

Gesellschaft für Selbstspielende Musikinstrumente EV: Dr Jürgen Hocker, Heiligenstock 46, 51465 Bergisch Gladbach, Germany.

Musical Box Society International (MBSI): New Members' Registration, Box 297, Marietta, Ohio 45750, USA.

Nederlanse Pianola Vereniging (NPV): M. R. Graus, Korte Dijk 10, 2871 CB Schoonhoven, Netherlands.

Perforons la Musique: Présidente, Lorraine Alessy, 27 Rue Labat de Savignac, 31500 Toulouse, France.

Reed Organ Society: President, Mr James Bratton, 2907 South Sidney Court, Denver, Colorado 80231, USA.

FURTHER READING

Joining any of the societies listed above will give members access to the books produced on this wide-ranging subject, but the better books, containing many excellent illustrations, are listed below. All were available at the time of writing. Many other good books have been written on this subject but are now out of print; they may still be available in local reference libraries.

Bowers, Q. David. *Encyclopedia of Automatic Musical Instruments.* 1972; reprinted twelve times. 1008 pages on all types of instruments. Available from Vestal Press, PO Box 97, Vestal, New York 13851-0097, USA.

Bullied, H.A.V. *Cylinder Musical Box Design and Repair.* 1987. Two volumes, 234 and 290 pages. Available from Vestal Press, PO Box 97, Vestal, New York 13851-0097, USA, or via the Musical Box Society of Great Britain.

Ord-Hume, Arthur W.J.G. *The Musical Box.* 1995. 340 pages, fully illustrated. Available from the Library of Mechanical Music and Horology, 24 Shepherd's Lane, Guildford, Surrey GU2 6SL.

Ord-Hume, Arthur W.J.G. *The Musical Clock.* 1995. 352 pages, fully illustrated. Available from the Library of Mechanical Music and Horology, 24 Shepherd's Lane, Guildford, Surrey GU2 6SL.

Most of the museums and societies also have a selection of books, tapes and CDs available, as well as materials for restoration and new paper music rolls or musical box discs for sale.

Those looking for old original pianola and organ rolls and associated items can find them in a twice yearly postal auction run by the Player Piano Group, or three times a year from Post Bid Enterprise, 39 Sydner Road, Stoke Newington, London N16 7UF.

PLACES TO VISIT

The following is a small selection of the many collections which include mechanical musical instruments of different kinds. Collections are listed each year in the various society journals. It is advisable to contact them before making a visit to check the opening times.

Forest of Dean Organ Museum, Springfields, Hawthorns Cross, Drybrook, Gloucestershire GL17 9BW. Telephone: 01594 542278.

Keith Harding's World of Mechanical Music, The Oak House, High Street, Northleach, Gloucestershire GL54 3ET. Telephone: 01451 860181.

Mechanical Music and Doll Collection, Church Road, Portfield, Chichester, West Sussex PO19 4HN. Telephone: 01243 785421.

Mechanical Music Museum, Blacksmith's Road, Cotton, Stowmarket, Suffolk IP14 4QN. Telephone: 01449 613876.

The Museum of Entertainment, Rutland Cottage, Millgate, Whaplode St Catherine, Spalding, Lincolnshire PE12 6SF. Telephone: 01406 540379.

The Musical Museum, 368 High Street, Brentford, Middlesex TW8 OBD. Telephone: 0181-560 8108.

The Nickelodeon Collection, Ashorne Hall, Ashorne Hill, near Warwick CV33 9QN. Telephone: 01926 65144.

Paul Corin's Magnificent Music Machines, St Keyne Station, St Keyne, Liskeard, Cornwall PL14 4SH. Telephone: 01579 343108.

Penny Arcadia, The Ritz Cinema, Market Place, Pocklington, East Yorkshire YO4 2AR. Telephone: 01759 303420.

Rye Treasury of Mechanical Music, 20 Cinque Ports Street, Rye, East Sussex TN31 7AD. Telephone: 01797 223345.

St Albans Organ Museum, 320 Camp Road, St Albans, Hertfordshire AL1 5PE. Telephone: 01727 869693.

Thursford Collection, Thursford Green, Thursford, Fakenham, Norfolk NR21 0AS. Telephone: 01328 878477.

Turners Musical Merry-Go-Round, Newport Pagnell Road, Wootton, Northampton NN4 0HU. Telephone: 01604 763314.